I0105856

Amazing Extinct Animals Timeline

David R Morgan

illustrated by Kateryna Shchufan

A2Z PRESS

Amazing Extinct Animal Timeline

This is a work of fiction.

Text and Illustrations copyrighted

by David Morgan ©2021

Library of Congress Control Number: 2020912467

All rights reserved. No part of this book may be

reproduced, transmitted, or stored in an information retrieval

system in any form or by any means,

graphic, electronic, or mechanical without prior written

permission from the author.

Printed in the United States of America

A 2 Z Press LLC

PO Box 582

Deleon Springs, FL 32130

bestlittleonlinebookstore.com

sizemore3630@aol.com

440-241-3126

ISBN: 978-1-946908-50-6

Dedication

To Bex and Toby,
Who are amazing
and for whom my love
will never end!

This Book Belongs To :

_____

10,000 BC: This is an amazing
extinct animals' timeline.
What an absolute shame it has
been to lose creatures so fine.

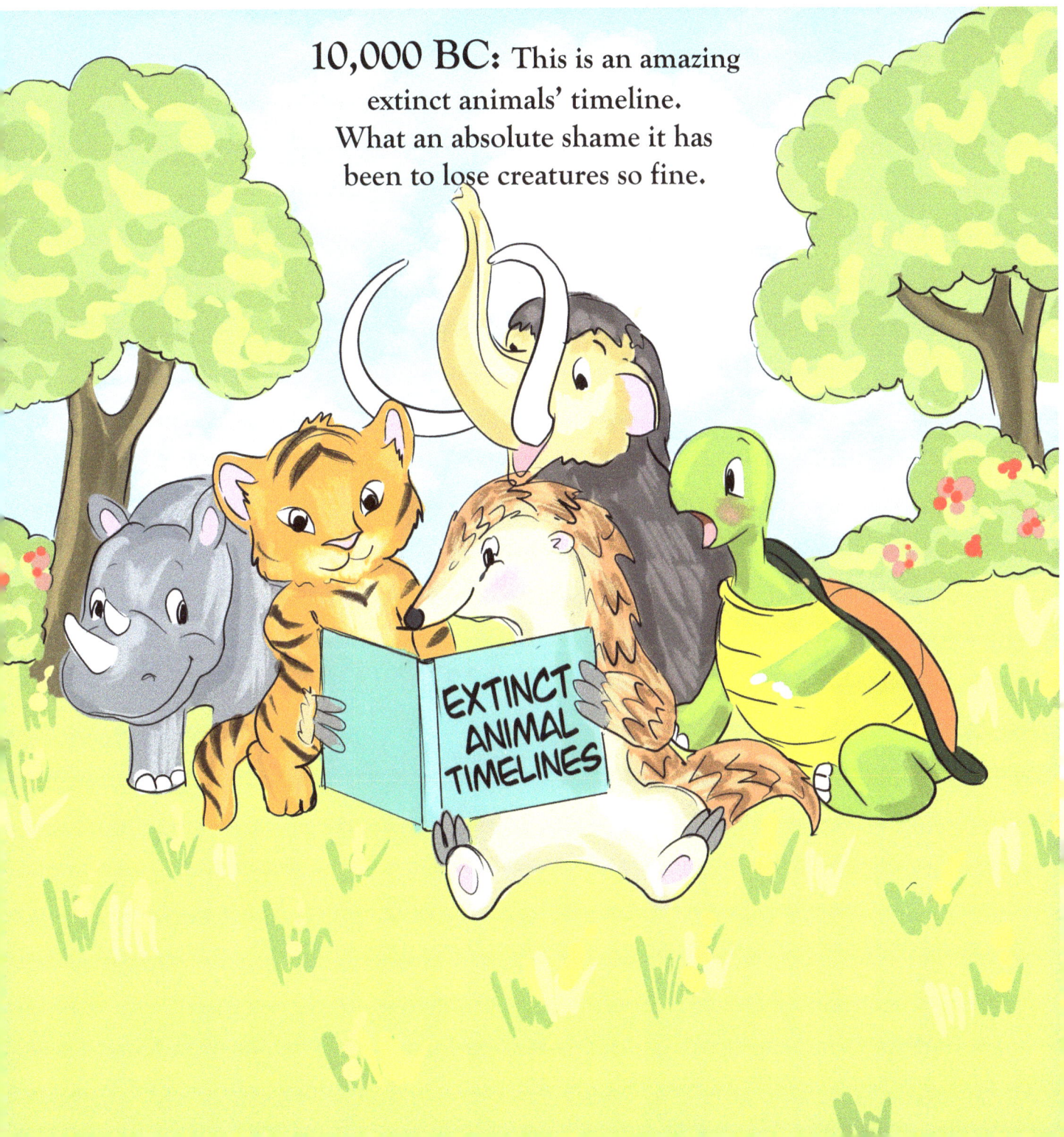

Since 10,000 BC, the Smilodon-
known as the Saber Tooth Cat,
Can no longer be found
in our world!
IMAGINE THAT!

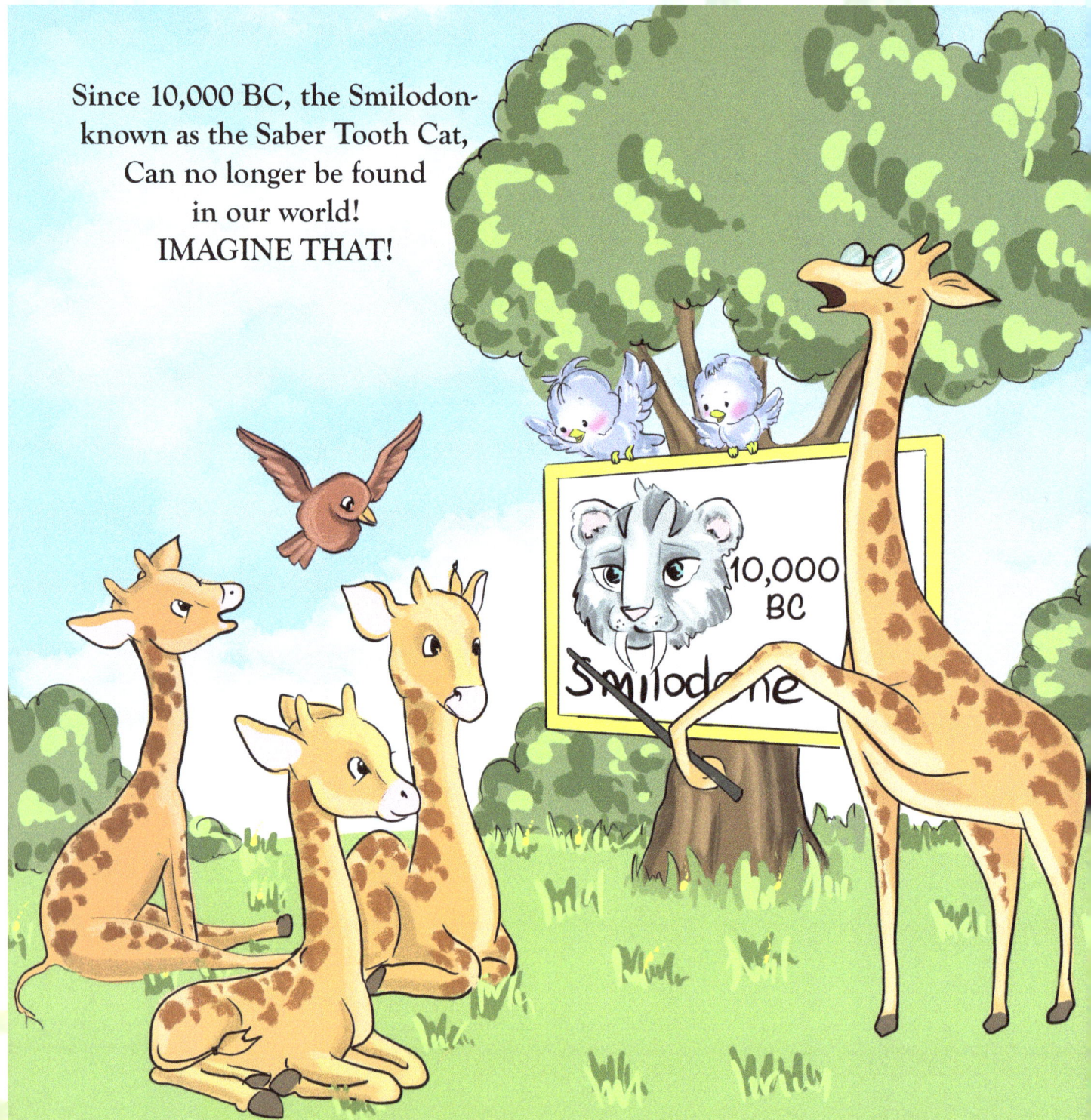

5,000 BC: The Great Irish Elk was the largest ever living deer, But sadly, in 5,000 BC, they were no longer here.

calendar
5000 Bc

calendar
5001 BC

They stood eight feet tall and,
had antlers that were 12 feet wide,
We know the last Elk stood alone,
In Ballybetagh Bog, near Dublin, and cried.

2,000 BC: Allowed us to see the Woolly Mammoth of the Ice Age,
But they are no longer anywhere—not in the wild and not in a cage.

2000 BC Woolly Mammoth

They were so majestic. Some were 12 feet tall with their shaggy hair,
And long curved tusks. Huge herds of this Mammoth roamed everywhere.

1400 AD: The marvelous Moa lived in New Zealand and no where else at all,
They were a large flightless bird and some grew to 11 feet tall.

They had not a wing among
'em but could run very, very fast,
But in 1,400 AD they say
the precious Mao's race was the last.

1768 AD: As we move on, we will go to the deep seas now,
Where we would have met the Steller's Sea cow.

They large sea mammals were 30 feet
long and 10 tons in weight,
And, OH, so friendly! But this
slow swimmer left us in 1768.

1852 AD: There was a small flightless bird only around three feet tall known as the Great Auk, They were excellent swimmers - so impressive that penguins would squawk!

The Great Auk was such a
sensational sight, but in 1852,
And to our misfortune,
has vanished from view.

1870 AD: In Africa, near the Atlas Mountains there,
Lived the impressive 10 feet tall Atlas Brown Bear.

ATLAS
BEAR

They were so sure-footed, climbing
the mountains that they scaled,
But 1870 was the end
of the Atlas Bear's tale.

1870

1883 AD: There once was a Quagga
that was a plains zebra, it is said,
The Quagga only had stripes
on its neck and on its head.

Once, there were so many roaming
around the Great Karoo to see,
But the Quagga were seen
no more after 1883.

1905 AD: And living in Japan,
the Honshu Wolf was petite,
Only 32 inches from its nose to
its tail, running around
on very small feet.

With their reddish ash color,
they were the smallest wolf and so clever,
But in 1905, they howled their last cute howl....forever!

1936 AD: The terrific Tasmanian Tiger was a marsupial carnivore, and in New Guinea and Australia, it's wolf's head was what you saw,

6 1/2 FEET LONG

They had stiff tails and bodies
of a dog that was 6 1/2 feet long,
And tiger stripes on their backs
and a   kangaroo pouch,
but in 1936, they were all gone!

1943 AD: Did you know that up until 1943, there was a Toolache Wallaby
That looked a lot like a Kanga and was a lovely, lively sight to see.

So ashy brown with a pale yellow underbelly and a tail of grey,

1943

and black faces and forearms, oh, why did they have to fade away?

1970

1970 AD: From the huge land mass of Russia to Turkey, the Caspian Tiger was as delightful an animal as could be,

They were nearly 7 feet in length and loved their habitat,
But in 1970, there were no more Caspian Tigers , and that's that!

WE SAID SO LONG
IN 1970

2008 AD: Until the 2008, the cute Caribbean Monk Seal, at nearly 11 feet tall, was a very big deal.

They were brown or grey in
color, but it all has come to an end,
For they are no longer with us—
no longer everyone's friend.

2011 AD: And everyone knows it is utterly preposterous,
That in 2011 we lost the wonderful Western Black Rhinoceros!

They stood 12 1/2 feet at the shoulder and ambled along, with two horns –the back one was shorter and the front one was five feet long!

2012 AD: The last Giant Pinta Island tortoise, Lonesome George, was 120 years old , He was the last of his kind and died in 2012 we are told.

HOW TO HELP SAVE
THE ANIMALS

And what are the next timeline dates we may have here?
We really do not want any more lovely creatures to disappear.

We hope everyone will help
save the critters we love so much,
Like pangolins and polar
bears and giraffes and such.

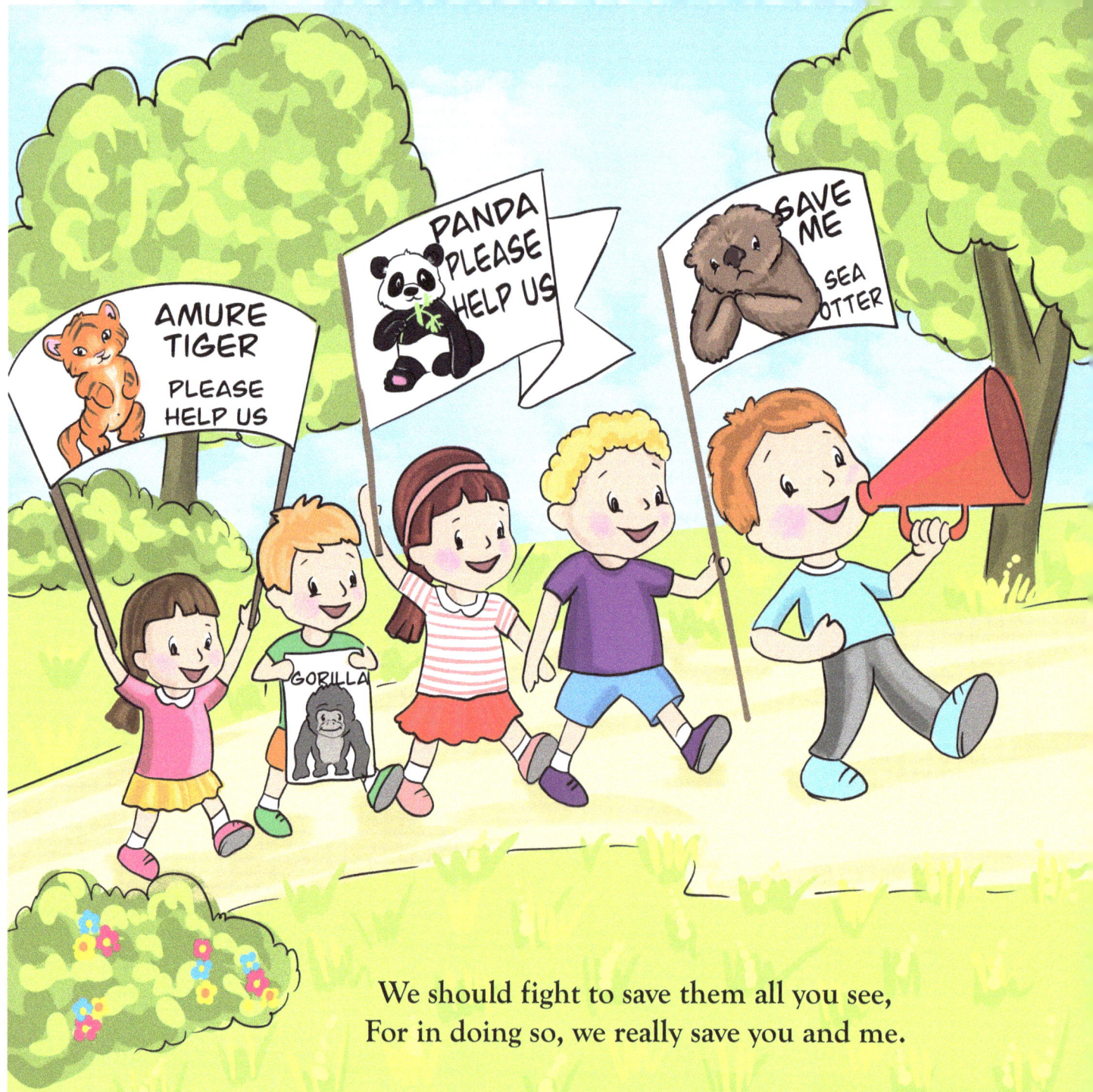

We should fight to save them all you see,
For in doing so, we really save you and me.

And together they saved everyone happily every after.

Wildlife - is everywhere but the world is always changing. Animals we see today may be in danger of being lost. It is estimated that 27,000 different animals, fish, reptiles, amphibians and more that we know about are at risk for extinction.

Wildlife conservation is how we protect wild animals and where they live in order to prevent them from becoming extinct.

The threats to wildlife are:

1. **Loss of their habitat** (homes). If animals have no place to live, they are lost. We live in a world where we take away the forests and jungles to make room for people and the animals have no homes.
2. **Taking animals** or fish at a rate faster than they are able to have babies to replace the ones taken - like too much fishing or taking too many bears.
3. **Pollution and poisons** - chemicals in the air and water can injury animals and fish or cause their loss. Even chemicals used for help with pests can be harmful.
4. **Climate change**. Increase in temperatures, melting ice sheets, changes in rain patterns, severe lack of rain, more frequent heat waves, storm intensification, and rising sea levels are some of the effects of climate change that change where the animals and fish live and can cause their loss.

Help

Species conservation -is conserving specific animals and reptiles - for instance: the leatherback sea turtle - the largest turtle in the world and one without a hard shell - is in danger. They are found in the ocean but have lost where they lay eggs, their eggs are eaten by others, and pollution in the sea are what are causing their decreased numbers and threatening their loss. Now, everyone in the world is trying to help save them.

Habitat conservation is ways we protect where animals live Some animals live everywhere and some in specific places. Habitat conservation usually sets aside protected areas like national parks or nature reserves. Elephants have these in Africa. Even when an area isn't made into a park or reserve, it can still be monitored and maintained. Red-cockaded woodpecker is a bird- in danger of being lost and they live in a different type home –they live in holes in tree cavities they dig out in the trunk. In an effort to increase woodpecker numbers, artificial cavities (that are essentially birdhouses planted within tree trunks) were installed to give woodpeckers a place to live.

An active effort is made by the US military and workers to maintain this rare habitat used by red-cockaded woodpeckers.

Some Endangered Ones:

Sea Otter

Siberian Tiger

Silky Sifaka

Whooping Crane

Sir Lankan Elephant

Saiga Antelope

Red Panda

Red Crowned Crane

Pangolin

White Rhino

Numbat

Gorilla

Monarch Butterfly

Lion

Kakapo

Snub-Nosed Monkey

Blue Whale

Aye Aye

Amur Leopard

Orangutan

David R Morgan lives in England. He is a talented full-time teacher and writer.

He has written music journalism, poetry and children's books. His books for children include: 'The Strange Case of William Whipper-Snapper,' three 'Info Rider' books for Collins, and 'Blooming Cats' which won the Acorn Award and was animated for television. He has also written a Horrible Histories biography: 'Spilling The Beans On Boudicca' and stories for Children's anthologies.

For the last four years he has been working on his Soundings Project with his son Toby, performing his own poetry/writing to Toby's original music. This work can be found on YouTube, Spotify, and Soundcloud.

Other Books by David R. Morgan

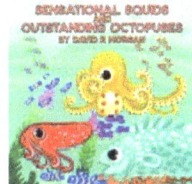

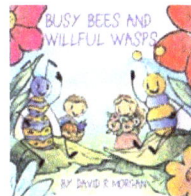

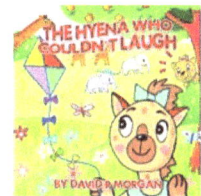

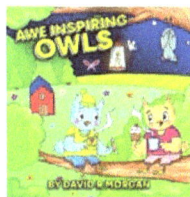

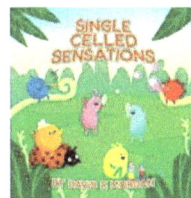

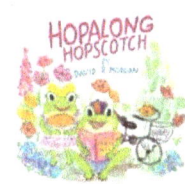

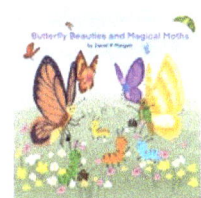

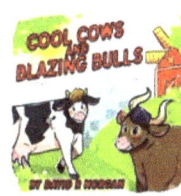

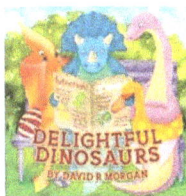

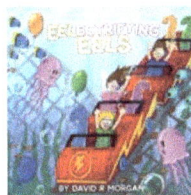

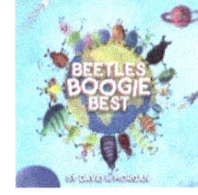

Ants are FANTastic

SENSATIONAL SQUIDS AND OUTSTANDING OCTOPUSES
BY DAVID R MORGAN

BUSY BEES AND WILLFUL WASPS
BY DAVID R MORGAN

SNAILS AND SLUGS SLIMY SUPERSTARS
BY DAVID R MORGAN

THE HYENA WHO COULDN'T LAUGH
BY DAVID R MORGAN

AWE INSPIRING OWLS
BY DAVID R MORGAN

Wonderous Whirring Whirring Worms
by David R. Morgan

SINGLE CELLED SENSATIONS

HOPALONG HOPSCOTCH
DAVID R MORGAN

Butterfly Beauties and Magical Moths
by David R Morgan

STUNNING SNAKES ARE HAPPY HISSERS
BY DAVID R MORGAN

Turtles AND Tortoises ARE Tremendous

COOL COWS AND BLAZING BULLS
BY DAVID R MORGAN

FABULOUS FROGS AND TERRIFIC TOADS

The Bookshop Cafe

DELIGHTFUL DINOSAURS
BY DAVID R MORGAN

ELECTRIFYING EELS
BY DAVID R MORGAN

RUNAWAY RAGTIME

CRABS ARE INCRABABLE

BEETLES BOOGIE BEST

And many more to come!

A2Z Press LLC

A2Z Press LLC
published this work.
A2Z Press LLC is a
publishing company
created by Terrie Sizemore
for the purpose
of publishing literary works by new
and aspiring writers. All content is
G-rated. We welcome your submissions
of ideas for children's literature as well
as adult and self-help topics.
Science and medicine, holidays and
other interesting topics are all welcome.
Submit queries to sizemore3630@aol.com or
PO Box 582
Deleon Springs, FL 32130

www.ingramcontent.com/pod-product-compliance
Lightning Source LLC
Chambersburg PA
CBHW042333030426

42335CB00027B/3323